M000300376

THE REFLECTION GUIDE TO THE

IMPACT CYCLE

WHAT INSTRUCTIONAL COACHES SHOULD DO
TO FOSTER POWERFUL IMPROVEMENTS IN TEACHING

Copyright © 2017 by Jim Knight

All rights reserved. No part of this book may be reproduced or transmitted in any form or by any means, electronic or mechanical, including photocopying, recording, or by any information storage and retrieval system, without permission in writing from the publisher.

Library of Congress Cataloging-in-Publication Data

The Reflection Guide to The Impact Cycle: What Instructional Coaches Should Do to Foster Powerful Improvements in Teaching.

Jim Knight, Jennifer Ryschon Knight, Clinton Carlson

Published by Corwin, Thousand Oaks, California
Printed in the United States of America
Cover design by Clinton Carlson

TABLE OF CONTENTS

INTRODUCTION

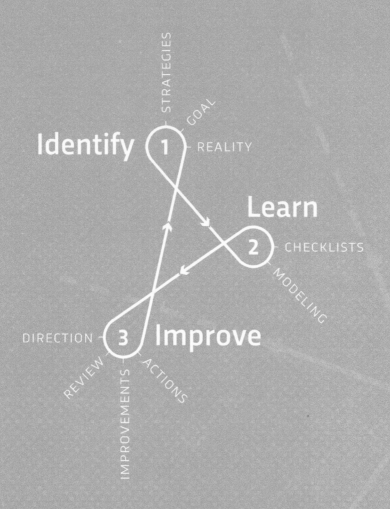

THE IMPACT CYCLE

Transformation.
Deep learning.
Achieving personal bests as a way of being.
Efficiency without loss of quality.

Making the difference for another person (a teacher, a student, or a friend) between loss of hope or the courage to overcome obstacles and experience the satisfaction of success. Being the change you want to see in the world and then actually changing the world. Who among us doesn't aspire to experience each of these things in our professional—and personal—lives? As educators, we hold these hopes for our students, for our colleagues, and for ourselves.

Instructional coaching is one of the most effective ways to improve teaching and learning in any instructional setting and, as a result, many schools have coaching programs in place. Instructional coaching honors the humanity of all involved in the learning process, and when the Impact Cycle is used to provide structure, focus, and responsible accountability to the coaching process, exciting gains can be made in your practice and—as a result—in student learning. In the words of one teacher who was coached through the Impact Cycle, "You will find that you aren't 'leaving behind' students when you adhere to these principles."

If you are a "solitary" coach feeling alone and uncertain of what the next steps are to move your practice forward, or if you are a leader of coaches in your school and need a simple, effective model to implement as you try to get everyone on the same page, then this little guide will be your best friend.

The Impact Cycle Reflection Guide is intended to serve you in several ways. First, it will serve as your slides and notes if you are participating in an Impact Cycle workshop as presented by Jim Knight or one of our other colleagues here at the Instructional Coaching Group .

Second, it will help guide you along in your personal or group study of the Impact Cycle. We have structured this guide to be conversational and user-friendly. You will note that prompts for reflection are sprinkled throughout the chapters when key concepts related to the Mother Book (as we fondly call *The Impact Cycle*) are discussed. The placement and type of reflections vary by chapter as appropriate to the flow of content in *The Impact Cycle*.

Third, it can serve as your go-to resource covering the most essential aspects of the Impact Cycle in an easy-to-find format.

As with everything created by the Instructional Coaching Group, this product is iterative. What you hold in your hands right now is just one iteration—perhaps it is the second, third, or fifteenth version of this book. For this reason, we welcome you to write us at **hello@instructionalcoaching.com** to share your experience using this book and provide any feedback you may have it for possible use in a future iteration.

WHAT DOES IT MEAN TO IMPROVE?

CHAPTER

////////////////////

1

> "Coaching done well may be the most effective intervention designed for human performance."
>
> ////////////////
>
> ATUL GAWANDE
> *Personal Best*
> The New Yorker, 2011

WHAT IS INSTRUCTIONAL COACHING?

An instructional coach partners with teachers to help them improve teaching and learning so their students become more successful. They do this by:

» helping the teacher analyze current reality

» setting goals

» identifying and explaining teaching strategies to hit goals

» providing support until the goals are met.

REFLECT

How is our definition of an instructional coach similar or different from your definition of an instructional coach?

....

....

....

....

....

Referring to Devona's story on page 3 in *The Impact Cycle*, what are some ways you could...

listen to your collaborating teacher?

....

....

....

affirm your collaborating teacher?

....

....

....

come alongside and support your collaborating teacher?

....

....

....

In what ways would you like to improve as a listener?

....

....

....

....

What are some ways you might be more affirming?

....

....

....

....

What do you do to come alongside and offer support to a particular teacher?

What are some effective ways to be supportive of your collaborating teacher?

Are there strategies you could employ to assist you in reaching your professional goals as a coach?

In the book *Better Conversations*, the following strategies are suggested:

» Being a witness to the good
» Treating others as equals (which is to say, others count as much as you do even though your expertise may be different than theirs)

Do you believe these strategies are critical to effective coaching practice?

Teachers as Partners

How instructional coaches interact with others is as important as what they do. Effective instructional coaches see their collaborating teachers as professionals and as the ultimate decision makers about what and how they will learn. We suggest that coaches guide their behavior by the following seven partnership principles.

The Seven Partnership Principles

//////////////////////

1. EQUALITY

Instructional coaches and teachers are equal partners; each voice counts the same.

REFLECT

How often do you tell your collaborating teacher what to do?

....
....
....
....
....

Consider the following meanings of faith. What does it mean to "have faith" in the teachers you're working with?

....
....
....
....
....

FAITH
- » A strong feeling of trust or confidence in something or someone. *Longman Dictionary of Contemporary English*
- » Complete trust or confidence. *Cambridge English Dictionary*
- » Trust/Belief/Confidence/Conviction
- » Trust: to allow credit, to believe someone is good or honest.
- » Allow others a chance. *Archaic*

Are you able to empathize with your collaborating teacher? Do you understand some of the things that make the teacher afraid, uncertain, hopeful, or happy?

....
....
....
....

Do you know what drives your collaborating teacher?

....
....
....
....

2. CHOICE

Coaches who act on the principle of choice position their collaborating teachers as the final decision makers, as partners who choose their coaching goals and decide which practices to adopt and how to interpret data.

Forming solid partnerships and creating an energizing learning environment requires autonomy. Anything less is energy draining. People should have a choice in what learning path is best for them at which point in time, in setting their own goals in relation to that, in deciding how they will learn and how to measure growth, and in choosing who they wish to come alongside them as a partner, mentor, or coach.

As coaches, we would want these things for ourselves, and we can give no less to the people with whom we work. We believe that part of changing the world is, as Mahatma Gandhi said, being the change we want to see, and that involves modeling what it is to be a true partner. In some organizations, true partnership has been denied for so long that people no longer know how to be a partner, how to make real choices, how to operate with confidence instead of fear, and how to see beyond positions to the persons who fill them.

Do you collaborate with teachers who say, "Just tell me what to do"? If so, what can you do to help them think and act more freely and independently?

....

....

....

....

"Coaching can increase focus and capacity, reduce overwhelm and dependency, and drive engagement and impact. But even with the best of intentions, today's busy managers find themselves defaulting to an old-school management approach: tell them rather than ask them; solve it for them rather than help them figure it out."
///////////////,

MICHAEL BUNGAY STANIER
The Coaching Habit, 2016

In modeling and embodying the partnership principles (especially equality and choice) in their work with their collaborating teachers and others, coaches have a powerful opportunity to be leaders who usher in the best kind of culture change. Rather than working from coercion or manipulation, coaches work to be hospitable and invitational, postures that allow for choice.

Manipulation: people are handled or controlled unfairly or unscrupulously and denied autonomy.

Partnership (invitation/hospitable posture): people are offered the opportunity to learn; they are encouraged and autonomously choose the right course for themselves.

Peter Block has said that, "If we can't say no, our yes means nothing." (*Stewardship,* 1993) In light of that, can meaningful transformation happen when people have no choice?

....

....

....

....

Coaching isn't just about improving instruction for students' sakes; it is very personal for both the coach and the teacher. The process is about cultivating a deep awareness of our practical reality and being able to choose to evaluate it, set goals, and reach personal bests in an ascending spiral of proficiency and professionalism. In other words, as we become our best, others benefit, and we create an empowering, free space—and invite others into that with us—rather than staying in a comfortable, yet limiting, box.

Autonomy—choice—is critical for the teacher, the coach, and perhaps more important, the students.

Consider what could happen when we live and coach without fear (and, therefore, without the need to coerce others). Perhaps we would be modeling what it looks like to live in freedom regardless of the limiting situations we find ourselves working within. When we allow others to act autonomously by honoring their right to say no to options that seem like the best course of action to us, but not to them, might we be able to preserve relationships and let them know we are available in the future if they change their mind or new challenges arise?

REFLECT

Do you gain something by keeping people dependent on you?

....

....

....

....

....

What is the benefit of telling people what to do? How easy is it for me to let others make their own decisions?

....

....

....

....

....

Am I willing to let teachers make their own choices even when they don't choose what I would choose? Could I support them in that place and encourage their growth by being a witness to the good?

....

....

....

....

....

....

Coaches who follow the principle of voice expect to learn from their collaborating teachers, and the teachers feel safe expressing what they think and feel and have confidence their opinion matters to the coach.

Many people have become used to the fact that their voice is not welcome. As a result, they may speak but say nothing. Or, they may not speak much, if at all. While there are things you can do to empower others, they may not have the courage or faith to act on that empowerment until they come to see you are a safe person they can trust.

When leaders empower others, they create the psychological space necessary for others to exercise self-determination and experience meaning, competence, and results in their work and personal lives. As coaches, we can create a psychologically safe environment that facilitates our collaborating teachers' ability to respond to and exercise their empowerment in the following four ways:

1. **Self-determination.** Empowered people feel that they have freedom, independence, and discretion over their work activities.
2. **Meaning.** People who feel empowered care about their work and believe that what they do is important.
3. **Competence.** Empowered people are confident about their ability to perform the work well and have a capacity to grow with new challenges.
4. **Impact.** Empowered people view themselves as active participants in the organization; that is, their decisions and actions have an influence on their own and others' success. (paraphrased from *Organizational Behaviour: Essentials*, 2e, MaMcShane & Van Glinow, 2008, p. 107)

Freedom is an invitation that requires a response; we continually create freedom with our empowered responses and actions.

The saying goes, "You can lead a horse to water, but you can't make it drink." As coaches, we provide water, and we do not judge others if they choose not to work with us. We understand that if people feel beaten down after years of unprofessional treatment, they may need a while to regain faith in others and confidence in their own voices.

As coaches, our goal is to help the teachers and students we work with become empowered once again. Operating from the partnership principles is how we do that.

REFLECT

What can you do to encourage your collaborating teachers to tell you what they are really thinking? Does your collaborating teacher feel safe with you?

....
....
....
....
....
....

Do you display a peaceful patience by asking one question at a time and waiting for the other person to answer the question completely before you follow up with another question?

....
....
....
....
....
....

What behaviors shut down a person's voice?

....
....
....
....
....
....

"Tell less and ask more.
Your advice is not as good
As you think it is."
////////////////

MICHAEL BUNGAY STANIER
The Coaching Habit, 2016

Consider the tongue-in-cheek haiku to the left about allowing space for another's voice:

....
....
....
....
....
....
....

4. DIALOGUE

Coaches who foster dialogue balance advocacy with inquiry; they actively seek out others' ideas, and they share their own ideas in a way that makes it easy for others to share what they think. Dialogue sets up instructional coaches as thinking partners with their collaborating teachers.

According to Michael Bungay Stanier, coaching often focuses on a "project, a person, or a pattern of behaviour. " (*The Coaching Habit*, 2016) For an instructional coach, the project could be working with a teacher on setting a goal and exploring strategies to achieve the goal. In terms of the person, instructional coaches value the personhood of teachers and show that by working with them respectfully through their commitment to the partnership principles.

Finally, with regard to patterns of behaviour, an important part of the instructional coaching process is looking at videos to gain a clear picture of reality as patterns and habits that may have been unconscious actions are revealed. In short, a commitment to dialogue is critical to effective coaching because the coach and teacher are working together on the goal (the project) while respecting one another, growing as people, and identifying and improving patterns of behaviour when working through the Impact Cycle.

Dialogue is enabled by the psychological safety created by the partnership principles of choice and voice. Without the ability to think and share ideas, coaching will not be effective. Coaches do not impose their views or opinions, dominate, or control. Instead, they focus the conversation on what is learned from the video, identifying a goal, strategies that can be used to reach the goal, and what they can do to refine and continuously improve as they move together through the Impact Cycle.

REFLECT

What are the best ways to balance advocacy with inquiry?

....

....

....

....

....

....

Are you actively seeking out your collaborating teacher's ideas?

Have people spoken of you as domineering or controlling?

Are you willing to shut down your certainty that you're right so you can give courage, support, and empowerment to your collaborating teacher and make space for his or her voice?

Are you interested in what your collaborating teacher is saying?

Award-winning instructional coach Delia Racines' own coach taught her that in every complaint there is a hidden request. Can you hear the request hidden in a complaint?

5. REFLECTION

Much of the pleasure of professional growth involves reflection on what we learn. An effective instructional coach creates space for reflection for themselves and their collaborating teachers. When coaches collaborate with teachers by co-creating ideas in reflective conversation, both teachers and coaches often find those conversations to be engaging, energizing, and valuable, and they feel encouraged.

All of the preceding partnership principles create and support a psychologically safe space for reflective conversation. If people are going to make meaningful changes, they need time to reflect.

Reflection requires time and autonomy. As a coach, how can you provide your collaborating teachers the time and autonomy they need for reflection?

6. PRAXIS

People who engage in praxis apply knowledge and skills to their work, community, or personal lives after reflection. When coaches act with the goal of praxis in mind, they make sure that coaching is productive, meaningful, and helpful to teachers and students.

Praxis is a funny-sounding word that sounds a lot like practice—and it is practice, but it's practice that is coupled with reflection on learning before action, during action, and after action.

The Impact Cycle is grounded in—and enables and guides—praxis. In the Identify phase, we reflect on what the video or audio recording tells us about the reality of our current practice and imagine and set a powerful, student-focused goal. Then, in the Learn phase, we consider different strategic options to help us achieve the goal and reflect on how each strategy could work in our context. Finally, as we enter the Improve stage of the Impact Cycle, we are immediately and constantly involved in practicing and then stepping back and reflecting on the practice and how it could be improved or tweaked to better serve our goal. After reflecting on our practice, we try again and reflect again on how things went until we reach our goal.

The beauty of the Impact Cycle is that it is simple without being simplistic, and it can be applied to almost any learning situation (personal or professional) to help people get better at what they do. To engage in coaching is to commit to trying to be the best we can be.

7. RECIPROCITY

Reciprocity is the inevitable outcome of an authentic partnership because partnership is as much about shared learning as it is about shared power.

For the instructional coach, partnership goes beyond shared power to the joy of shared learning. This involves being intentional about creating an environment where shared learning can thrive by adhering to all the partnership principles, most obviously, choice, voice, and dialogue. The chart below illustrates how the partnership mindset differs from the top-down mindset.

TOP-DOWN	PARTNERSHIP
Compliance	Commitment
People *outside* the classroom know what students need	People *inside* the classroom know what students need
One size fits all	One size fits one
Constructive feedback	Dialogue
Coach does most of the thinking	Teacher does most of the thinking
Judgmental	Nonjudgmental
Teachers have lower status than coaches	Teachers have equal status with coaches
Accountable to leaders	Accountable to students

REFLECTION

These questions help you gauge whether you are more committed to top-down compliance or partnership:

Do you think you know more about what the students need than the teacher does?

....
....
....
....

Or, do you trust that the teacher knows what her students need?

....
....
....
....

Do you believe every student or teacher is served by the same approach to learning?

....
....
....
....

Or, do you embrace the fact that every teacher and student has unique needs and are you committed to meeting those needs as well as you're able?

....
....
....
....

Are you focused on giving feedback or advice?

....
....
....
....

Or, are you focusing on engendering dialogue?

....
....
....
....

Are you doing all of the thinking, relying totally on your own understanding and committed to your own preconceived ideas of what you think your collaborating teacher ought to do?

....
....
....
....

Or, are you working to cultivate conditions that generate dialogue to ensure you are thinking together with your collaborating teacher?

....
....
....
....

Are you focused on judging or learning?

....
....
....
....

Or, are you keeping an open mind, seeking to understand your collaborating teacher?

....
....
....
....

Do you believe that your collaborating teacher cannot possibly count as much as you do (be equal to you) because she has different expertise?

....
....
....
....

Or, do you work together with the teacher humbly, as an equal, believing her voice is as important as your own, with the goal of empowering and encouraging her?

....
....
....
....

Are you most concerned about what your supervisors think of you?

....

....

....

....

Or, are you most concerned with partnering with teachers to reach student-centered goals that transform instruction and learning?

....

....

....

....

An Introduction to the Coaching Cycle

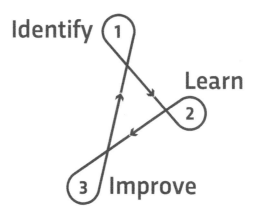

THE IMPACT CYCLE

The Impact Cycle consists of three phases: Identify, Learn, and Improve.

A critical starting point for any coaching endeavor is to gain an objective, clear picture of current reality by creating a video or audio recording of the collaborating teacher and her students. The video objectively and without judgment captures our current practice and helps us to see our blind spots. It stands as a third thing, which enables us to get out of our own way by creating a way to view and consider our practice from different angles. It helps us to get outside of ourselves and see what others—most important our students— see and experience when we do what we do.

When we are able to see the current reality of our practice in a safe, objective way, we may see, as Jackie and Melanie did in the example offered in *The Impact Cycle*, that what we thought was most important isn't that important and something else needs our immediate attention.

Three Approaches to Coaching: Facilitative, Dialogical, and Directive
///////////////////////.

It is very important for leaders to adopt the right approach to coaching for the kind of change they hope to see. Indeed, choosing the wrong coaching model can cause problems—like choosing a plumber to wire your house. For that reason, we divide coaching into three approaches: facilitative, directive, and dialogical.

FACILITATIVE COACHING:

The Sounding Board.
These coaches encourage teachers to share their ideas openly. They refrain from sharing their own expertise or suggestions with respect to what a teacher can do to get better. This approach may be used in all types of situations, so it has the potential to address issues that dialogical or directive coaching is not able to address. The relationship is based on equality. *Primarily inquiry*

DIRECTIVE COACHING:

The Master and the Apprentice.
In many ways, directive coaching is the opposite of facilitative coaching. The directive coach has special knowledge, and his or her job is to transfer that knowledge to the teacher. In an instructional coaching scenario, directive coaches work from the assumption that the teachers they are coaching do not know how to use best practices. The relationship is respectful, but not equal.

Coach does most of the thinking

Coaches expertise is the focus of the session

DIALOGICAL COACHING:

The Partner.
Dialogical coaches balance advocacy with inquiry. That is, they share strategies and options for improvements provisionally and help teachers describe precisely both what it is they want to achieve and how to get there. Furthermore, they go beyond mere conversation to dialogue, where thinking is done together and neither teachers nor the coaches are expected to withhold their

Deep coaching

Coach shares expertise but dialogically

teacher is ultimate decision maker!

IMPACT RESEARCH LAB

"thinking together"

"bouncing ideas off of each other"

ideas. The relationship is equal. Effective instructional coaches are usually dialogical coaches. Therefore, this is the approach we use as we move through the Impact Cycle.

An instructional coach understands the three types of coaching and recognizes that an instructional coach works primarily as a dialogical coach. Although dialogue and thinking together with the collaborating teacher drive the coaching process, the instructional coach is aware of and understands the two other forms of coaching and is able to use any of the three approaches as situations may dictate. Nevertheless, directive coaching is used minimally—if at all—by an effective instructional coach.

REFLECT

When a teacher you're working with implements a strategy that you wouldn't have picked or implements a strategy in a radically different way than it was designed to be used, are you OK with saying, "Well, let's see if we can hit the goal!" and trusting that the Impact Cycle will surface what does and doesn't work?

....
....
....
....

As an Impact Cycle instructional coach, our approach to coaching is dialogical. In what scenarios would it be more effective to draw on the techniques of facilitative or directive coaching models?

....
....
....
....
....
....
....

Consider when those models are best used for coaching that is not instructional in nature.

....
....
....
....

"The facilitative coach focuses on inquiry, using questions, listening, and conversational moves to help a teacher become aware of answers he already has inside himself. The directive coach focuses on advocacy, using expertise, clear explanations, modeling and constructive feedback to teach a teacher how to use a new teaching strategy or program with fidelity. The dialogical coach balances advocacy with inquiry" (p. 16).
///////////////
The Impact Cycle

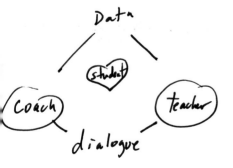

Deep Learning,
Deep Coaching
////////////////////.

Deep Learning

"Real learning gets to the heart of what it means to be human. Through learning we recreate ourselves. Through learning we become able to do something we were never able to do. Through learning we reperceive the world and our relationship to it. Through learning we extend our capacity to create, to be part of the generative process of life. There is within each of us a deep hunger for this type of learning."
///////////////.

PETER SENGE
The Fifth Discipline: The Art and Practice of the Learning Organization, 1990

At its heart, coaching is about striving to become the best version of ourselves and being committed to continuous and measurable improvement. Think about the feeling you get when you gain a new competency and how motivating that is. That is the very thing deep coaching taps into—the desire we all have to be the very best version of ourselves.

Deep learning changes us in unmistakable ways. Deep learning can come from positive or negative experiences.

What is one deep learning experience you have had?

....
....
....
....
....
....

Was the learning the result of a positive or a negative experience?

....
....
....
....

How did the experience change you?

....
....
....
....

What steps did you take as a result?

....
....
....
....

What was the outcome?

....

....

....

....

....

When instructional coaching is done well, it empowers the learner to experience deep learning.

Deep Coaching vs. Surface Coaching

As described in *The Impact Cycle*, when instructional coaches do surface coaching, they provide teachers with resources, offer supportive comments, model lessons, provide quick observations, and share quick feedback. In other words, surface coaching does not involve teachers in the deep work of setting student-focused goals and collaborating until those goals are met, and it usually only involves superficial reflection and results in very little sustained change.

When coaches enable deep coaching, on the other hand, they guide teachers through a reflective process that involves setting goals, identifying teaching strategies to be implemented to reach those goals, collaborating, and adapting teaching and learning until the goals are met. Deep instructional coaching uses the Impact Cycle.

REFLECTION QUESTIONS

Has your coaching practice been more like surface coaching or deep coaching?

....

....

....

....

....

....

Do you want to do more deep coaching?

....

....

....

....

What do you need from your administration or others to help you be more effective in enabling deep learning?

....

....

....

If you don't get what you need from others, how can you empower yourself to be the most effective coach you can be?

....

....

....

FURTHER REFLECTIONS

Here is what we know: Top-down, strict authoritarian models of coaching and learning generally won't work. Top-down models foster resistance and dehumanize teachers and students by limiting autonomy and empowerment. Very little is more deeply personal than our minds and how and what we learn. For that reason, very little is more important than partnering with learners in ways that respect their humanity.

We live in a world that seems hell-bent on embracing everything that opposes partnership. Empowered instructional coaches can be leaders who usher in a more humane way of interacting. Instructional coaches can be leaders who model the change so desperately needed in education and in the world at large.

Coaching is a deeply humane, creative and beautiful act. To be beautiful, something must be of a high standard, or excellent. The interesting thing about beauty is how it "protests darkness," as artist and former high school teacher, Sara Groves, has put it. A beautiful life and practice inspires others and invites them into a community of hope, empowerment, freedom, and possibility.

In this way, instructional coaching can be "beautifully practiced" as the coach listens and leads (without rushing or forcing) to remove chaos and replace it with clarity.

Not only does your school need you, the world needs you, Coach. It needs you to coach well, to coach beautifully, and to help lead us into a kinder, gentler, more purposeful tomorrow by embodying that tomorrow today.

REFLECT

What kind of coach do you want to be?

....
....
....
....
....
....
....
....
....
....

What do you hope to accomplish as an instructional coach:

... In your school?

....
....
....
....
....
....

... In the world?

....
....
....
....
....
....

What outward behaviors, attitudes, and habits are the hallmarks of a great dialogical (instructional) coach?

....
....
....
....
....
....
....
....

What do you most hope to learn about the instructional coaching process as you engage with the Impact Cycle?

....

....

....

....

....

....

....

What part of being an instructional coach gives you the most anxiety?

....

....

....

....

....

....

....

How could you benefit from having a coach yourself?

....

....

....

....

....

....

....

....

....

....

....

....

....

....

....

....

EXERCISE:

Identify Your Mysteries.

//

As you look through the chapter summaries on pages 27-29 in *The Impact Cycle*, identify some things that at this point are unclear to you. What would you like to have a solid understanding of when you have finished working through each chapter of *The Impact Cycle*?

CHAPTER 2

....
....
....
....
....

CHAPTER 3

....
....
....
....
....

CHAPTER 4

....
....
....
....
....

CHAPTER 5

....
....
....
....
....

Consider the following questions from the position of an *administrator*:

What type of coaches do you want in your school or district?

....

....

....

....

....

If you want dialogical coaches—highly effective instructional coaches—and the outcomes associated with them, what will you do to support the coaches?

....

....

....

....

....

Will you make certain that the coach has the time to focus on coaching instead of saddling one person with the impossible job of being a part-time coach while handling a plethora of other responsibilities?

....

....

....

....

....

Are you willing to accept that it would be unfair to judge the effectiveness of a coaching program if that coach/es is/are not allowed the time needed to build relationships with teachers and begin to enroll them and coach them through the Impact Cycle?

....

....

....

....

....

....

Are you willing to work with a professional coach for your own growth so you have empathy for the teachers and coaches in your district, showing them that you care by "walking the talk"?

....

....

....

....

....

....

Consider the following questions from the position of a **coach of coaches:**

What kind of coach do you want to be?

....

....

....

....

....

....

....

....

....

....

Are you ready to have a conversation with the leadership in your school/district about what you and your coaches need to be successful?

....

....

....

....

....

Are you committed to being coached yourself?

....

....

....

....

....

....

Consider the following questions from the position
of an *instructional coach:*

What kind of coach do you want to be?

....
....
....
....
....
....
....
....
....
....
....

What support will you need and want from your director of
instructional coaching?

....
....
....
....
....
....
....
....
....
....
....
....
....

GOING DEEPER

As a professional, you are committed to always learning. Which
book in the Going Deeper section of Chapter 1 in *The Impact Cycle*
are you committed to reading this quarter?

....
....
....
....
....
....

Do you have a conversation partner or another coach or group of coaches with whom to form an informal professional learning community?

....

....

....

....

....

....

If you formed such a group, consider reading one of the books on the list and then making time together to each share key learning and insights and/or summaries from each book. Would this be helpful?

....

....

....

....

....

....

NOTES

....

....

....

....

....

....

....

....

....

....

....

....

....

....

....

....

....

....

GETTING A CLEAR PICTURE OF REALITY

CHAPTER

////////////////////

2

"The juxtaposition of vision (what we want) and a clear picture of current reality (where we are relative to what we want) generates what we call creative tension: a force to bring them together, caused by the natural tendency of tension to seek resolution. The essence of personal mastery is learning how to generate and sustain creative tension in our lives."

////////////

PETER SENGE

Summarizing Robert Fritz's theory of creative tension in *The Fifth Discipline: The Art and Practice of the Learning Organization,* 1990

The Impact Cycle is a deceptively simple process involving three stages: Identify, Learn, and Improve. The Cycle positions collaborating teachers as the ultimate decision makers in a process leading to powerful improvements in student learning and wellbeing. With a coach's help, teachers analyze video and student data, set powerful goals for the coaching cycle, identify what teaching strategies to implement to hit the goals, and problem solve with their coach until goals are met.

Instructional coaches who use the Impact Cycle understand that their main task within that cycle is to help teachers achieve their goals. Teachers, because they make the important decisions about what happens in their classrooms, see the Impact Cycle as a process designed to help them achieve their goals for their students.

Step 1

/////////////////////

Get a clear/shared picture of current reality to create a baseline for measuring growth and movement toward goals.

Gaining a clear picture of reality is important because:

- » It gives a shared, objective understanding of what is happening in a teacher's classroom.
- » The focus that arises from having a clear picture of reality (and, ultimately, a goal) saves teachers and coaches time.
- » It shifts teacher and coach out of talk and into action.

After viewing the video recorded in the classroom, ask yourself ...

What is going well?

....

....

....

....

Where is there room for improvement?

....

....

....

....

What is the ideal situation you'd like to see in your classroom and/or students?

....

....

....

....

"To confront reality is to recognize the world as it is, not as you wish it to be, and have the courage to do what must be done, not what you'd like to do."

/////////////////////

BOSSIDY AND CHARAN
Confronting Reality, 2004

The Illusion of Objectivity

Because of perceptual errors, we tend to view the world through an illusion of objectivity. We think we see ourselves and the world around us accurately but, in reality, we usually see and understand things through many filters that color our perceptions.

Confirmation bias: Our natural tendency to color our perceptions of reality by consciously or unconsciously seeking data that support our assumptions about the world around us.

Habituation: Our tendency to become desensitized to any experience, positive or negative, that we experience repeatedly.

Primacy effect: Our tendency for our first experiences with someone or something to bias us in favor of a particular impression of that person or thing.

Recency effect: Our tendency for our last experiences with someone or something to bias us in favor of a particular impression of that person or thing.

Stereotypes: Prejudging people as having the characteristics of a group (often negative), which blinds us to the unique characteristics of individuals.

To help us cut through our illusions, we need safe, nonjudgmental tools. There are three options to consider:
1. Video recording (the easiest and most powerful!)
2. Learning from students
3. Gathering observation data

Overcoming the Illusion of Objectivity

Part 1: Video Recording the Lesson

There are several issues to consider before making video a part of your coaching practice: trust, choice, ownership, filming, kind of camera, where to point the camera, the length of the recording, and how to watch the video.

"It's hard for people to watch themselves. It's hard for me to watch myself, but video has transformed everything. Sometimes teachers will come to me and say, I think I really need to work on this, and then they watch their video and change [their minds] completely based on what they watched. When teachers stand in front of a classroom, they don't always have that perspective of what's really happening in their classroom. But, when I set that video up in the back of their classroom, they can watch themselves, or look at a lesson through the kids' eyes, and can see what I see. You can't give them that picture without the video. I don't think I could coach without video, now."
//////////////

JACKIE JEWELL
Instructional Coach
Othello, Washington

TRUST.

A culture of trust needs to be in place for video to be embraced. In order for people to trust individuals or organizations, the following five factors must be in place.

The Five Factors of Trust
1. Honesty
2. Reliability
3. Competency
4. Warmth
5. Genuine concern for the good of others (charity)

CHOICE.

Invite, don't force; use the teacher's camera, begin with audio if that is what the teacher prefers.

OWNERSHIP.

Create psychological safety by giving the teacher total control over the video and how it will be used.

FILMING.

The instructional coach can operate and control what the camera is to focus on, or the camera can simply be set up in the back of the room.

KIND OF CAMERA.

The simplest cameras to use are the ones in smartphones and tablets. However, you could also use a Go Pro camera or a Swivl to support the camera. Keep in mind the camera needs to have enough memory to capture the video, and the microphone needs to be sensitive enough to record the sounds in the classroom.

WHERE TO POINT THE CAMERA.

The teacher can decide based on what he or she wishes to observe more closely.

THE LENGTH OF THE RECORDING.

Twenty minutes is a good start. Less than 20 minutes typically is not enough time to see the arc of what is going on in the classroom. If the lesson is less than 50 minutes, recording the whole class is ideal. After a goal has been set, record the part of the class specifically related to the goal.

"If teachers don't want to do the video, the problem isn't the video—the problem is trust."
////////////////

INSTRUCTIONAL COACHES
Beaverton, Oregon
Team consensus on why teachers won't use video recordings.

WATCHING THE VIDEO.

Coach and teacher should watch the video separately and then discuss it with each other afterwards. To get the most out of the video, use the following forms from *The Impact Cycle*: How To Get The Most Out Of Watching Your Video, Watch Your Students, Watch Yourself.

VIDEO AND STUDENTS.

We've found that the presence of the camera is generally not a distraction to students but, of course, no two classes are the same.

WHY TEACHERS SHOULD BE RECORDED.

Video is an extremely effective tool for helping inform and improve practice. Video recordings powerfully capture interactions between students and teachers.

A Review of How to Use Video

A thorough study of how to use video to enhance professional learning was offered in *Focus on Teaching: Using Video for High Impact Instruction* (Knight 2014), but it may be helpful to quickly revisit the most critical behaviors for using video when entering the coaching cycle at the first stage, Identify.

1. **Establish trust.** For the use of video to flourish, teachers need to feel psychologically safe. They need to know they won't be penalized for mistakes and that the video itself is in their control at all times.

2. **Make participation a choice.** As suggested by the partnership principles of autonomy and choice, teachers should not be forced to use video. Instead, they should be invited to use a powerful tool for learning and improving. Learning is unlikely if teachers are forced to do a video recording against their will.

3. **Focus on intrinsic motivation and safety.** Instructional coaches encourage, empower, inspire, and invite others to set goals that help them achieve a personal best while improving student engagement and learning. The self-awareness produced by video can spur us to want to improve to be the best version of ourselves. However, when coaching is tied to extrinsic rewards, the intrinsic motivation for getting better is decreased and sometimes erased.

4. **Establish clear boundaries.** Boundaries increase psychological safety and focus. Some important boundaries to consider include (a) focusing on data, (b) being nonjudgmental, (c) respecting the complex nature of teaching, (d) being positive, (e) being respectful, (f) being supportive, and, (g) offering suggestions for improvement only after being asked, and then only provisionally.

5. **Walk the talk.** If administrators (in addition to coaches) want others to take the brave step of watching themselves on video, they need to walk the talk by being willing to watch their own practice on video as well. Thus, administrators might record and view workshops they provide, meetings they lead, and conversations they engage in.

6. **Go slow to go fast.** When coaches enroll collaborating teachers into the Impact Cycle, they should begin with the teachers who are the informal leaders within the school. Coaches should start work quietly, simply, and effectively with a small number of people who are interested and inspired to keep improving their practice. Coaches should emphasize that video-based professional development is always the collaborating teacher's choice and point out that it's okay to start with a simple audio recording if that is what the teacher is the most comfortable with. Audio is not as powerful as video. However, although it is a small beginning, it is a very worthwhile one.

7. **Use a simple camera on a tablet or smartphone.** Simple is good. Initially, setting the camera up in the back of the room for a birds-eye view is best. Later, depending on the goal and what you're trying to learn, you can adjust the position of the camera.

8. **Consider district policy around the use of video.** Consent may not be an issue if the video will never be made public. Generally speaking, this should never be the case for video used in the coaching cycle anyway.

REFLECT

Are you willing to watch yourself conducting your professional practice on video, reflect on your current reality, set goals for improvement, and, as needed, be willing to secure a coach for yourself?

What quarterly or monthly goals can you set for yourself around your own practices?

....

....

....

....

....

....

....

Are you willing to follow up with other video recordings to monitor your progress on the way toward your goal?

....

....

....

....

....

Are you up for continuing to make and work to achieve new goals?

....

....

....

....

....

Is it fair to ask your teachers (or coaches) to do something you are unwilling to do yourself?

....

....

....

....

....

NOTES

Getting the Most Out of Watching Your Video

//.

GOAL:

Identify two sections of the video that you like and one or two sections of video you'd like to further explore

....
....
....
....
....
....

GETTING READY:

Watching yourself on video is one of the most powerful strategies professionals can use to improve. However, it can be a challenge. It takes a little time to get used to seeing yourself on screen, so be prepared for a bit of a shock. After a little time you will become more comfortable with the process.

○ Find a place to watch where you won't be distracted.

○ Review the Watch Yourself and Watch Your Student forms to remind yourself of things to keep in mind while watching.

○ Set aside a block of time so you can watch the video uninterrupted.

○ Make sure you've got a pen and paper ready to take notes.

WATCHING THE VIDEO:

○ Plan to watch the entire video at one sitting.

○ Take notes on anything that catches your attention.

○ Be certain to write the time from the video beside any note you make so that you can return to it should you wish to.

○ People have a tendency to be too hard on themselves, so be sure to really watch for things you like.

○ After watching the video, review your notes, and circle the items you will discuss with your coach (2 you like, and 1 or 2 you would like to further explore).

○ Sit back, relax, and enjoy the experience.

Watch Your Students

//

After watching the video of today's class, please rate how close the behavior of your students is to your goal for an ideal class in the following areas:

Students were engaged in learning
(at least 90% engagement is recommended)

Not Close O—O—O—O—O—O—O Right On
          1 2 3 4 5 6 7

Students interacted respectfully

Not Close O—O—O—O—O—O—O Right On
          1 2 3 4 5 6 7

Students talked about learning an appropriate amount of time

Not Close O—O—O—O—O—O—O Right On
          1 2 3 4 5 6 7

Students rarely interrupted each other

Not Close O—O—O—O—O—O—O Right On
          1 2 3 4 5 6 7

Students engaged in high-level conversation

Not Close O—O—O—O—O—O—O Right On
          1 2 3 4 5 6 7

Students clearly understand how well they are progressing (or not)

Not Close O—O—O—O—O—O—O Right On
          1 2 3 4 5 6 7

Students are interested in learning activities in the class

Not Close O—O—O—O—O—O—O Right On
          1 2 3 4 5 6 7

COMMENTS

....

....

....

....

....

....

....

DATE

WORKSHEET:

Watch Yourself

//

After watching the video of today's class, please rate how close your instruction is to your ideal in the following areas:

My praise to correction ratio is at least a 3 to 1 ratio
_____

Not Close O—O—O—O—O—O—O Right On
            1 2 3 4 5 6 7

I clearly explained expectations prior to each activity
_____

Not Close O—O—O—O—O—O—O Right On
            1 2 3 4 5 6 7

My corrections are calm, consistent, immediate,
and planned in advance
_____

Not Close O—O—O—O—O—O—O Right On
            1 2 3 4 5 6 7

There was very little wasted time during the lesson
_____

Not Close O—O—O—O—O—O—O Right On
            1 2 3 4 5 6 7

My questions at the appropriate level (know, understand, do)
_____

Not Close O—O—O—O—O—O—O Right On
            1 2 3 4 5 6 7

My learning structures (stories, cooperative learning, thinking devices, experiential learning) were effective
_____

Not Close O—O—O—O—O—O—O Right On
            1 2 3 4 5 6 7

I used a variety of learning structures effectively
_____

Not Close O—O—O—O—O—O—O Right On
            1 2 3 4 5 6 7

I clearly understand what my students know and don't know.
_____

Not Close O—O—O—O—O—O—O Right On
            1 2 3 4 5 6 7

COMMENTS

....
....
....
....

DATE

"To record a lesson and not record what the teacher does is like recording a batter during a baseball game and not recording the pitcher. We learn more by seeing more, and the best way to learn about how we teach is to watch how we teach."
//////////////
The Impact Cycle, 2017

Overcoming the Illusion of Objectivity

Part 2: Learning From Students

"One of the most powerful ways to get a clear picture of reality in a classroom is to ask students for their opinions about what they are experiencing."
//////////////
The Impact Cycle, 2017

Students are the consumers of education, so their voices should be listened to most carefully. Sadly, too often their voices are not heard.

Asking students about how learning is proceeding in a class has several advantages:
- » Students are the only people with first-hand knowledge of how learning is proceeding.
- » The most effective goals are student-focused goals, so it only makes sense to seek out students' opinions about their learning goals.
- » Involving students communicates deep respect for them.
- » When students have a say in their learning, they are more likely to own the process of learning.
- » Just like adults, students want to have a voice and choice over their learning.

"All human beings want their voices to matter. We like giving our opinions and offering ideas. We want to be the subject for our own activities, not the objects of someone else's."
//////////////
QUAGLIA AND CORSO
Student Voice, 2014

There are many ways teachers and coaches can listen to students:
1. informal conversation
2. interviews
3. writing prompts and exit tickets
4. listening to them
5. reviewing their work.

LEARNING FROM STUDENTS, PART A:
Informal Conversations
(a) Outside of class, strike up a conversation with a student about his or her experiences in the class; and (b) Make it a goal to talk to two students in every class every day about their experiences inside and outside of school.

Questions to Initiate Daily Conversations With Students
- » What's the best thing about coming to this class?
- » What's the worst thing about coming to this class?
- » What are you most excited about these days?
- » How comfortable do you feel saying what you think in this class?
- » What could make this class more interesting for you?
- » Is this class too easy, too hard, or just right for you?
- » What should be changed in this school to make this a better school for you?
- » What do your friends say about our school?

Interviewing Students

» One-to-one interviews with students are most effective for generating a candid discussion.
» To get a clear understanding of what students think of the class, we suggest interviewing about 20% of the students.
» The students can be interviewed by either the coach or the teacher.

Questions for Students in Grades 5-12

» How would you say the class is going for you?
» How engaged are you in class?
» Tell me a bit about your goals for school, life, work.
» What roadblocks are you encountering as you try to achieve your goals?
» What can our class and our school do better to help you achieve your goals?
» When do you feel comfortable speaking up in class?
» What could be changed about our class to help you learn more?
» What else can you tell me about how this class can become a better learning experience for you?

Questions for Students in Grades K-4

» What do you like about school?
» What don't you like about school?
» What do you wish you could do more of in school?
» Describe what the perfect school would look like for you.
» What do your friends say about the school?
» If you were the teacher, what would you change about the way things go in the class?
» Is there anything you want to tell your teacher or the school principal?

LEARNING FROM STUDENTS, PART C:
Writing Prompts and Exit Tickets

Another way to get feedback from students is through writing prompts and exit tickets. Students should be encouraged to share what they think without any fear of retribution or being graded on their comments. Here are some ideas.

> » Have students journal or write a paragraph about what it feels like to be in this class.
> » Consider having a Conversation Journal where students and teachers write back and forth about how things are going every week (no judgment, no grades—this is a safe place to communicate).
> » Educators love the word engagement, but it can be a bit abstract for some students. To get a sense of student engagement, consider this question instead: How could today's lesson be changed to be more interesting to you?
> » In order to quickly gauge how the students are feeling about the class, have several sets of emoji cards ready to go. Students can choose the emoji that best suits how they feel their learning is going, and drop it into a basket.
> » Use one of the Student Attitude Surveys in the Impact Cycle Data Toolkit at the end of *The Impact Cycle*.

LEARNING FROM STUDENTS, PART 4:
Listening to Students

The three steps to assuring students they have been heard:

ASK → LISTEN → RESPOND

Giving students a voice does not mean anything if it stops there. The way you prove that you care about what students are saying is to ask them what they think and then listen and respond.

Most importantly, after asking the students to give you feedback, follow up by responding to their feedback. When students hear a thoughtful and genuine response to what they said, they know they've been heard and that their voice matters. Unless they feel like they've been heard and taken seriously, they'll stop offering meaningful information.

If you think about it, a class is a presentation of material with the teacher doing the presenting to an audience—the students. You ask them to fill out evaluation forms at the end of class, much like you would evaluate a presenter of a professional development training after his or her session. The next day, you can read a few of the exit tickets out loud or note themes from interviews conducted by the coach. But always, always, always protect students' anonymity. This lets the students know you hear them and you are taking their voice seriously by responding to their comments with good will and humility. Finally, asking students for their opinions and ideas is only helpful as long as you communicate to the students how you will act on what you hear.

LEARNING FROM STUDENTS, PART 5:
Reviewing Student Work

Another way to gain a clear picture of current reality in the classroom is to review the work being done by the students. There are a few ways to do this.

The coach and teacher together can look at recent work turned in by the students and identify major strengths and weaknesses.

Coaches can review recent student work for the teacher and summarize strengths and weaknesses by (a) applying criteria the teacher identifies as important, and (b) operating from a shared understanding of the elements of the criteria used to analyze the work.

Other ways to gather data include:
  » Using the chart paper method
  » Assessing reading skills by sitting beside the student and asking him to read a passage out loud.
  » Speaking quietly with students at their desks and asking questions like, "What are you learning right now?' or "Why is this learning valuable?"

Overcoming the Illusion of Objectivity

Part 3: Observation (Gathering Data)

When we talk about data with teachers, we ground the conversation in the partnership principles, which position the teacher as the person who will make the decisions about what data to gather. This does not mean that coaches silence themselves, but they share ideas provisionally and clearly. Coaches work with teachers for teachers and students, not for themselves.

Coaches should clarify how the observation will proceed before they observe to gather data.

Pre-Observation Conversation

ACTION

○ Take notes during the conversation.

○ Determine the desired form of feedback—(a) appreciation, (b) coaching, (c) evaluation, or (d) some other form.

○ Determine the purpose of the observation—(a) to get a clear picture of reality, (b) to establish a baseline for setting a goal, (c) to monitor progress toward a goal, or (d) some other purpose.

○ Explain the different kinds of data that can be gathered.

○ Determine which types of data will be gathered.

○ Determine the location, date, and time for the observation.

○ Determine whether or not it is OK for you to talk with students in the class.

○ Ask, "Is there anything I need to know about particular students or this class in general?"

○ Determine where you will sit and whether or not it is OK for you to move around the class.

○ Ask, "Is there anything else you want to ask me that you haven't asked yet?"

○ Determine how you will share data (e.g., face-to-face, via email).

○ Identify when and where you will meet to discuss data.

Take notes as seems useful. Use the following Observation Plan Form.

Observation Plan

PURPOSE OF THE VISIT	**NOTES**
○ To get a clear picture of reality	
○ To establish a baseline for setting a goal	
○ To monitor progress toward a goal	
○ Some other purpose:	

KIND OF FEEDBACK DESIRED	**NOTES**
○ Appreciation	
○ Coaching	
○ Evaluation	
○ Some other form:	

DATA TO BE GATHERED

○	Time on task	○	Respectful interactions
○	Experience sampling	○	Open vs. closed questions
○	Ratio of interaction	○	Right/wrong vs. opinion questions
○	Instructional and noninstructional time	○	Level of questions
○	Real learning index	○	Opportunity to respond
○	Ratio of interaction	○	Correct academic responses
○	Corrections	○	Different students responding
○	Disruptions	○	Teacher vs. student talk
○	Other:		

WHEN WILL I VISIT THE CLASS

LOCATION   DATE   TIME

Should I talk with students:

○ Yes   ○ No

SPECIAL INFORMATION ABOUT STUDENTS OR THE CLASS:

Where should I sit?

Is it OK for me to walk around the classroom during the lesson?

○ Yes   ○ No

Is it OK for me to talk with students during the lesson?

○ Yes   ○ No

OTHER INFORMATION I SHOULD KNOW:

How will I share data?

○ Face-to-face   ○ Via email   ○ Other:

NEXT MEETING

LOCATION   DATE   TIME

Stone and Heen (*Thanks for the Feedback: The Science and Art of Receiving Feedback Well, 2014*) write about three types of feedback, and it's important to clarify what kind of feedback the teacher would like:

» Appreciation—feedback on our successes
» Coaching—feedback that helps us get better (but coaches should not evaluate)
» Evaluation—feedback that tells us how we are doing in comparison to others or a standard

Confirm what the purpose of the observation will be:

» To get a clearer picture of reality?
» To establish a baseline for setting a goal?
» To monitor progress toward the goal?
» Some other purpose?

Explain the different kinds of data generally used in situations like this (time on task, experience sampling, instructional vs. non-instructional time, real learning index, ratio of interaction, corrections, disruptions, respectful interaction, types and kinds of questions, level of questions, opportunities to respond, correct academic responses, different students responding, teacher vs. student talk time):

» The coach provides an overview of the types of data
» The teacher decides what type to focus on

Determine when the observation will take place:

» What class could teach us the most?
» The teacher chooses!

Ask for specific information about the class or the students:

» Which parts of the class should observation be focused upon?
» Are there any particular students on which to focus?

Clarify what the teacher is comfortable with you doing while observing:

» Where is the observer supposed to sit or stand?
» Is it OK to walk around?
» Is it OK to talk with the students?

Remember, as a coach, you are a guest, so don't interfere with the learning process!

Determine how data will be gathered:

- » How data will be gathered depends on the focus of the observation
- » Use forms included in *The Impact Cycle* to help focus your observation (e.g., The 20-Minute Survey)
- » Use seating charts to help keep track of data

Finalize other details:

- » Confirm how data will be shared with the collaborating teacher—Will the teacher wish to see the data before the coaching conversation, or will she be OK having that conversation in the coaching session?
- » Where and when will the coach and teacher discuss the data?
- » Before closing the conversation, ask if there is anything the teacher would like to ask that hasn't been asked to this point.

MAKING IT REAL

Have you recorded any of your own presentations or yourself modeling strategies for use in your own professional coaching sessions?

....
....
....
....
....

Would you consider recording a conversation with your spouse or child?

....
....
....
....
....
....

As a coach, have you set up a time to video record yourself coaching so you can coach yourself or be coached by another coach or group of coaches?

....
....
....
....

Have you set up a time with other coaches to watch videos of teachers and practice your observational, data-collection skills?

....

....

....

....

GOING DEEPER

Which of the books listed in the Going Deeper section of *The Impact Cycle* would be most helpful for your practice?

....

....

....

....

....

....

....

....

....

....

....

....

....

....

....

....

....

....

....

....

....

....

....

....

....

....

NOTES

IDENTIFYING GOALS

CHAPTER

////////////////////

3

"...when it comes to altering behaviour you need to help others answer only two questions. First, is it worth it? ...And second, can they do this thing?"

////////////////////

KERRY PATTERSON
Influencer: The Power To Change Anything, 2008

After we have gained a clear picture of reality and have had a chance to reflect on what is going well and what could be improved, we are ready to set a powerful, student-focused goal.

Goals are essential for success. When teachers partner with coaches to set and meet measurable student goals, coaching improves instruction. When there is no goal, we run the risk that coaching will not have a lasting impact.

After studying the literature on goals, we discovered that the most powerful framework for setting a goal is the PEERS model, which we developed further via many iterations with coaches in Beaverton, Oregon, and Othello, Washington.

Setting a PEERS Goal

////////////////////////.

A PEERS goal is a goal that is powerful, easy (to implement), emotionally compelling, reachable, and student-focused.

"Simplicity is the ultimate sophistication."
///////////////
STEVE JOBS

POWERFUL

» Is the goal worth the time you will invest trying to reach it?
» Will the goal make a significant difference in students' lives and learning?

EASY

» Is the goal described in simple terms?
» Does the goal describe a clear destination and the shortest path to that destination?
» Does the collaborating teacher believe he or she (and the students) can reach the goal?

EMOTIONALLY COMPELLING

» Change involves how people feel and think, so to be compelling, a goal needs to speak to a person's emotions as well as his or her reason.
» When people don't change, it often is because they don't feel emotionally compelled to solve the problem.
» The coach helps teachers identify what part of the class worries them the most, or what they dislike the most about teaching, and uses that as a signifier of what could become an emotionally compelling goal.

REACHABLE

» Is the goal reachable? A goal provides hope if it can be reached.
» Is the goal clearly stated? Clarity dissolves resistance, according to Heath and Heath (*Switch*, 2010).
» Does the goal provide a vivid picture of what is possible? It's important to have a clear vision of what the class looks like as a result of achieving the goal.
» Does the goal spell out exactly what you want to achieve? This makes it less likely that your collaborating teacher will settle for less than is possible, and it also helps you chart your course of action.
» Are there clear strategies that could be used to reach the goal? Hope comes in knowing the goal can be reached and having a path to get there.

» Does the goal have a clear finish line? Can you precisely describe what will be different as a result of hitting the goal? Imprecise goals create frustration; clearly described goals build hope.

» What is the measurable finish line, and will it be clear how to measure progress toward the goal?

STUDENT-FOCUSED

» Does the goal provide clear feedback on whether or not the changes are making a difference for students? A student-focused goal provides clear feedback on whether or not the changes implemented by the teacher are making a difference where it counts: in the lives and learning of the students (embedded responsible accountability).

» What will be different for the student if the goal is met?

CHECKLIST:

 # PEERS Goals

//

A PEERS GOAL IS:

○ Powerful: Makes a big difference children's lives.

○ Easy: Simple, clear, and easy to understand.

○ Emotionally compelling: Matters a lot to the teacher.

○ Reachable: Identifies a measureable outcome and strategy.

○ Student-focused: Addresses a student achievement, behavior, or attitude outcome.

The Art of Questioning

//////////////////////

Reaching a Goal by Practicing the Art of Questioning via the Following Seven Practices:

SEVEN PRACTICES OF GOOD QUESTIONING

1. Create a welcoming environment
2. Build trust
3. Listen
4. Gain clarity
5. Ask for more
6. Learn rather than judge
7. Keep ourselves out of the answers

The Art of Questioning #1:

Create a Welcoming Environment

» What soothes—or stresses—your collaborating teacher?

» In what ways can you create an atmosphere that puts your collaborating teacher at ease? Make sure your coaching conversations take place in a comfortable, private space where it is unlikely you'll be interrupted.

» What are your collaborating teacher's likes and dislikes?

The Art of Questioning #2:

Build Trust

» It is difficult to respond authentically, if at all, to someone we do not trust.

» As a coach, it is critical to embody the Five Components of Trust:

1. Are you trustworthy, truthful, and fair? Do you need to change something to be perceived as more trustworthy?

....
....
....
....
....
....
....
....

2. Are you reliable? Are there responsibilities you can decline so you will have more time to be reliable? What rituals can you add to your day to help you be reliable?

....

....

....

....

....

3. Are you competent? Are you continually developing your professional skills and adding to your knowledge so you can better help people reach their goals? Are you practicing your skills; for example, by working through the Making It Real exercises at the end of each chapter in *The Impact Cycle*? Are you deeply learning the things that will make you an excellent coach?

....

....

....

....

....

4. Do you have a personality that exudes warmth? That is, are you kind? Are you slow to speak and quick to listen and gain understanding? Do you share authentic, positive information? Are you a good listener? Are you seeking to build emotional connections with the teachers you are collaborating with and hope to collaborate with in the future?

....

....

....

....

....

5. Do you convey an attitude of stewardship or benevolence (charity)? Do you have others' best interests at heart? How can you change so that you are less concerned with yourself and more thoughtful toward others?

....

....

....

....

....

Listen Well

> "If coaches don't listen carefully, they will struggle to coach effectively."
> ////////////
> *The Impact Cycle, 2017*

- Do you really want to hear what the other person has to say?
- Are you able to be completely present to others, and, if not, are you working to become more present?
- Is it possible to be a thinking partner with your collaborating teachers if you are not genuinely interested in what they have to say and are not listening carefully to understand where they are coming from?
- Do you believe you can learn from your collaborating teacher?

THE FOUR ELEMENTS OF BEING A GOOD LISTENER

1. Commit to listen. What is your collaborating teacher saying? Award-winning instructional coach Delia Racines has learned to "listen for the request in the complaint."
2. Make sure your collaborating teacher is at the center of the conversation. Ask: Am I allowing my partner to guide the conversation?
3. Pause to affirm before responding. Ask: Have I heard this correctly?
4. Don't interrupt too often. There are appropriate times to interrupt and help refocus the conversation.

THE THREE LEVELS OF LISTENING

1. Listen to what is said. Do you understand what your collaborating teacher is saying?
2. Listen for the inner voice—the deeper, real meaning in what people say that is hidden by using guarded language.
3. Be aware of the interview process. Keep in mind how much time is left for a particular coaching conversation. Are you staying focused on the targeted outcome for the conversation? Is the conversation moving too fast or is it too slowly?

The Art of Questioning #4:

Gaining Clarity

1. Ask one question at a time, and allow time and space for the collaborating teacher to respond. "Let silence do the heavy lifting" (Scott, 2002).
2. Ask for clarity on vague words or concepts or if you need to back track or in any way gain a better understanding of what your collaborating teacher is saying.

OTHER WAYS TO GAIN CLARITY

Ask yourself:

» Are you focused on the conversation, or are you drifting in and out?

» Do you have a clear understanding of what your partner is thinking and feeling?

» Are you giving adequate time for your partner to respond?

» Do you ask one question at a time and allow time for your conversation partner to form a response before you ask another question?

» Do you and your collaborating teacher have a clear understanding about what you both are speaking?

The Art of Questioning #5:

Ask for More

» Instead of asking "probing" questions (these are often perceived as uncomfortable), ask the AWE question: And What Else? (Michael Bungay Stanier, *The Coaching Habit*, 2016)

The Art of Questioning #6:

Learn Rather Than Judge

» Do you believe that your collaborating teachers are doing the best they can, given everything else they are dealing with right now?

» If you don't believe they're doing the best they can, how will that affect your relationship with them?

» Is there a way you can find the ability to work from the assumption that your collaborating teachers are doing their best so that your relating to them and your coaching will be more effective?

» Will your collaborating teachers recognize that you are on their side if you don't believe the best about them?
» Do you have a judging mindset or a learning mindset? If you have a judging mindset, should you work to change that to a learning mindset?

JUDGING MINDSET

» Judges others' thoughts, feelings, or situations
» Considers self an expert, regardless of experience
» Focuses on own role (which may lead to using a self-protective approach) and refuses to take the role of an outside observer, a researcher, or a reporter (unable to detach)
» Looks at the situation from one perspective: his or her own
» Fails to look for and find win-win solutions
» Is intolerant of self and others
» Fails to ask clarifying questions and just assumes he or she knows what the other person means
» Fights change aggressively most or all of the time

LEARNING MINDSET

» Responds without judging others' thoughts, feelings, or situations
» Considers self a beginner, regardless of experience
» Avoids focusing on self (which may lead to using a self-protective approach) and takes the role of an outside observer, researcher, or reporter (is able to healthfully detach)
» Looks at the situation from multiple perspectives, especially the respondent's
» Looks for win-win solutions
» Is tolerant of self and others
» Accepts change as a constant and embraces it

The Art of Questioning #7:
Keeping Ourselves out of the Answers

» Are you refraining from trying to shape your collaborating teacher's answers and decisions (manipulation)?
» Are you refraining from asking leading questions?
» Are you refraining from asking questions that are actually advice disguised as a question?

It is important to balance thinking about how you are practicing the art of questioning and keeping the collaborating teacher's words at the front of your mind. To become better at this, practice until you have made the art of questioning a habit from which you operate by default. The easiest and best way to do this is to video record your coaching conversations to see how you are adopting these habits and identifying which ones you still need to work on.

Use the following form to help guide your practice. You can use it by video recording conversations and reviewing the conversation with the checklist in hand.

Consider practicing one habit daily, or weekly, until you feel it is a natural part of the way you communicate. In addition, you might wish to review the Beliefs section in *Better Conversations*, as communicating from those beliefs naturally results in you becoming skilled at the art of questioning.

Listening and Questioning Effectively

TO LISTEN AND QUESTION EFFECTIVELY, I:

○ Make sure my conversation partner does most of the talking

○ Pause and affirm before I start talking

○ Don't interrupt (except when it is very helpful)

○ Ask one question at a time

○ Ask for clarification when I'm not certain what is being said

○ Ask, "And what else?"

○ Assume people are doing their best

○ Avoid leading questions

○ Avoid giving advice disguised as a question

The Identify Questions

/////////////////////////

The Identify Questions are a list of questions that coaches and our research team have developed, tested, and refined over time. They have proven to be powerful for structuring conversations that lead to the identification of a goal. When sitting down with a collaborating teacher (after reviewing a video) to set a PEERS goal, the Identify Questions are at the heart of the conversation.

"... [P]sychology is not just the study of pathology, weakness and damage; it is [also] about the study of strength and virtue."
/////////////////////

SELIGMAN & CSIKSZENTMIHALYI
2000

1. On a scale of 1-10, with 10 being the best lesson you've ever taught and 1 being the worst, how would you rank that lesson?

   Using a scaling question rather than an opinion question makes for a more constructive conversation by ...
   » focusing on how things ought to be
   » encouraging change
   » measuring change
   » confirming progress
   » providing a means of deciding priorities and next steps
   » showing teachers they are in charge of the coaching process

2. What pleased you about the lesson?
   » This question helps balance the conversation to include both what did and what didn't go well.
   » A negative view of reality is as ineffective as denial.
   » What went well can be a point of departure for getting better.
   » It is good to build on strengths—both teachers' and students'!

3. What would have to change to move the lesson closer to a 10?
   » This question grounds the discussion in reality while keeping the focus on a better possible future.
   » Keep the focus on what can be done, not on what isn't working.
   » Practice the power of visualization by describing exactly what it would look like if the students were acting in a way that promoted their learning.

"Suppose that tonight you go to bed—and you go to sleep as usual—and during the night a miracle happens—and the problem vanishes—and the issues that concern you are resolved—but you're asleep, so you don't know that the miracle has happened—so when you wake up tomorrow what will be the first things that tell you that the miracle has happened? How will you know that the transformation has occurred?"

/////////////

JACKSON AND MCKERGOW

The Solutions Focus: Making Coaching and Change Simple, 2013

» Describe the change you want to see in yourself and your students.

» Ask the "miracle question" to help clarify the solution:

4. What would your students be doing differently if your class were a 10?

» What do the students need?

» What would improve the students' wellbeing?

» Asking this question helps to avoid what Michael Bungay Stanier calls "the advice monster," (The Coaching Habit, 2016) and will help you to stay curious.

» Consider: Can you be comfortable as an instructional coach with the general ambiguity of asking meaningful questions as opposed to giving advice?

» The problems with advising instead of asking are (a) we alone are doing the thinking, and (b) we decrease our collaborating teachers' ownership of the solution and their commitment to change.

5. Tell me more about what that change would look like.

» This is a variation of the AWE question and provides more clarification on the change the teacher hopes to see in the classroom.

» The question provides a look at the classroom from a broader perspective before pinning down a goal and strategies.

6. How would we measure that change?

» If coaching is to succeed, there must be a finish line, a way to measure progress to know when we've reached the goal for which we are aiming. How do we identify the endpoint? Are we measuring a behavior? Achievement?

» Has the teacher created a clear vision and description of what will be different when the goal is met?

» Quantifying the goal helps the coach and collaborating teacher determine if the changes they are implementing are moving students forward.

» Progress toward the goal should be measured at least once a week to inform adjustments needed in order to stay on track.

» Can you describe clear goals that do not require (are measured by) a number?

7. Do you want that to be your goal?

» After working through the previous questions, the teacher is now ready to choose a goal that will make a real difference for students because she will know more clearly what it is she truly wants for the students.

» Ask again, what do you really, really want? Allow time for a thoughtful response.

» As a coach, be reminded that the coaching process must be fully guided by the teacher's concerns and desires.

» This question communicates that coaching is an act of service. As an instructional coach, then, ask: Do I see my job as an act of service?

8. If you could hit that goal, would it really matter to you?

» Unless the teacher cares deeply about the goal, she won't reach it.

» Think creatively and remain open to hearing what the teacher's most pressing concerns are.

» Does the goal hit the teacher in the gut? Does it feel right? If not, encourage the teacher to identify a more compelling goal.

9. What teaching strategy can you use to hit your goal?

» As a coach, do you have a deep understanding of a small number of high-impact teaching practices?

» Do you have an instructional playbook of those practices at the ready?

» Do you feel prepared with solid strategies and practices to offer the collaborating teacher?

» Are you willing to see the list of strategies and practices in the playbook as a sort of menu of options from which the teacher is free to choose? Remember: Coaching is not a top-down practice. So, before offering your own strategies, ask the teacher if she knows of a strategy she'd like to try first.

» Keep the dialogue going and keep in mind the importance of balancing inquiry with advocacy.

» Two heads are better than one!

"There is a difference between having expertise and showing up as the expert ...."
//////////////

LAURELIN ANDRADE
Instructional Coach
Salem-Keizer Public Schools
Salem, Oregon

10. What are the next steps?
- » What specific next actions do we need to take to move the cycle forward?
- » When and where will coaching occur?
- » What will happen during those sessions?
- » How will the teacher see and learn the strategy to be used?
- » When will the strategy be implemented?
- » When will data be gathered?

TIME AND GOAL-SETTING
- » On average, it takes a coach and teacher five to six hours to work through a cycle. However, it is counterproductive to set a time-bound goal because each situation is unique.
- » Trying to squeeze deep coaching into six weeks or stretch it out into a longer amount of time is not as sensible as simply continuing the coaching cycle until the goal is met.

MAKING IT REAL
- » Use the Identify Questions in every Impact Cycle.

- » Practice the coaching process with other instructional coaches.

- » Video record your coaching sessions with teachers and use the Listening and Questioning checklists to improve your coaching practice.

- » Self-coach once a week until the habit of Impact Coaching feels like second nature. Then, coach yourself once a month to maintain your skills and add new ones.

GOING DEEPER
With your coaching learning community, pick a book or books from the Going Deeper section in *The Impact Cycle* to study this month/quarter.

Coaching Planning

GOAL	PROGRESS	NEXT ACTIONS	WHEN	COMMITMENT LEVEL (1-5)
○	○			
○	○			
○	○			
○	○			
○	○			
○	○			
○	○			

Learn:

TEACHING STRATEGIES

CHAPTER

////////////////////

4

"We need a different strategy
for overcoming failure, one
that builds on experience
and takes advantage of the
knowledge people have but
somehow also makes up
for our inevitable human
inadequacies."

////////////////

ATUL GAWANDE
*The Checklist Manifesto:
How to Get Things Right
2010*

79 | CHAPTER 4

Many of us are drawn to become instructional coaches for the same reason: to share the strategies that have worked for us in the classroom. Over fifteen years of working with instructional coaches and educators have taught us that doing this it isn't as simple as we initially thought.

Through testing and refining we've identified three major ways for instructional coaches to share and teach teaching strategies: (a) by creating an instructional playbook, (b) by sharing checklists, and (c) by modeling.

IMPACT RESEARCH GROUP

1.

Strategies Can Be Shared and Taught by Creating an Instructional Playbook

To help teachers improve student learning and well being by improving instruction, the coach must be able to clearly describe a set of teaching strategies teachers can use to hit their goals. The Instructional Playbook describes these strategies using the following three tools:

a. a one-page list of high-impact teaching strategies

b. one-page descriptions for each of the strategies

c. checklists to help coaches describe the teaching practices contained in the playbook

A full Instructional Playbook, including one-page descriptions and checklists for each teaching strategy, is included in *The Impact Cycle: What Instructional Coaches Should Do To Foster Powerful Improvements In Teaching*.
////////////////////

Instructional Playbook

CONTENT PLANNING

Guiding Questions

Learning Maps

FORMATIVE ASSESSMENT

Specific Proficiencies

Checks for Understanding

Checklists

Rubrics

INSTRUCTION

Thinking Prompts

Effective Questions

Stories

Cooperative Learning

Authentic Learning

COMMUNITY BUILDING

Learner-Friendly Culture

Power With vs Power Over

Freedom Within Form

Expectations

Witness to the Good

Fluent Corrections

IMPACT RESEARCH LAB

High-impact teaching strategies list.

OVERVIEW:

Learning Maps

//

IN ONE SENTENCE:

A graphic organizer depicting the essential
knowledge, skills, and big ideas students are
to learn in a unit.

THE HATTIE CHECK:

Student Expectations 1.44; Teacher Clarity .75; Concept Mapping .75.
Students can use learning maps to review, monitor their learning,
and confirm understanding.
Learning maps are a form of concept map teachers can use to ensure their lessons are clear.

WHAT'S THE POINT?

Learning maps are powerful because their visual depiction of a unit
keeps students and teachers on track.
The map is an accommodation for students who struggle to take
notes, and it structures the beginning and ending of lessons.
Learning maps are living study guides that make connections explicit and support repeated review.

HOW ARE LEARNING MAPS USED BY TEACHERS?

Teachers should spend 25-40 minutes to introduce the unit through
an interactive discussion of the map on the first day of a unit.
Throughout the unit, the maps may be used as visual prompts for
conversations around advance and post-organizers.
Teachers should prompt students to record new information on
their maps as it is learned.
At the end of the unit, maps can be integrated into the unit review.

HOW ARE LEARNING MAPS USED BY STUDENTS?

Students use learning maps:
to take note of key information,
to frequently review and clarify their learning, and
as points of departure for classroom dialogue.

One-page strategy description.
/////////////////

CHECKLIST:

Learning Map

A QUALITY LEARNING MAP:

○ Answers all the guiding questions

○ Has a starting map with only the core idea, paraphrase, and subtopics

○ Has a complete ending map on no more than one page

○ Shows connections through line labels

○ Is organized according to the sequence of the learning in the unit

INSTRUCTIONAL PLAYBOOK

Example of a strategy checklist.

"If you can actually get everything
on one page—and not just editing
stuff out—that means the tool and
the process caused you to reflect
on what it is you do .... If you limit
the number of pages people have
to explain themselves, it forces
them to reflect first and think
about what they're trying to do."
///////////////

BILL JENSEN
*Simplicity: The New
Competitive Advantage, 2000*

ONE-PAGE LIST

The playbook begins with a clear list of the teaching strategies
contained within it, much like a simple menu from which a coach
can make a quick selection. It is only one page long to keep it simple
and user-friendly. A comprehensive list need not be a long list. It just
needs to contain high-impact teaching strategies that address the
most critical aspects of teaching, which we define as the Big Four:
content planning, formative assessment, instruction, and community building (classroom management).

One powerful way to create a list of strategies is for coaches to work
together to create a list of their best go-to strategies. The list is a
living document that is constantly adjusted to reflect only the most
powerful, simple-to-use practices. Therefore, it should be reviewed
at least once a year.

ONE-PAGE DESCRIPTION OF TEACHING STRATEGIES

Like the one-page teaching strategies menu, the summary for each
strategy is only one page long, providing an overview of the strategy,
so teachers can quickly decide if it is something that would be
worthwhile for a given situation. Much more detailed information
about the strategies is communicated by coaches through the use
of checklists during the Learn Stage of coaching.

2.

////////////////////////

Strategies Can Be Shared and Taught by Creating and Using Checklists

WHY USE CHECKLISTS?

- » They make it easy to remember, describe, and model instructional practices.
- » They help ensure deep knowledge of the content.
- » They reinforce knowledge of the practices and help the coach communicate them effectively.
- » For these reasons, checklists make up the bulk of the instructional playbook.

REFLECT

As a coach, are you continually learning, reading about strategies, and creating your own checklists?

....

....

....

....

Are you sharing them with others and asking others to share their lists with you?

....

....

....

....

Are you engaging in regularly refining the strategies and the checklists?

....

....

....

....

Are your books marked up and highlighted showing a running conversation with the author of the book/checklist/strategy?

....

....

....

....

FOUR REASONS WHY EXPLAINING STRATEGIES TO TEACHERS MAY FAIL— AND WHY CHECKLISTS HELP

1. The coach's description is too long or too detailed and lacks precision.
2. Teachers are overwhelmed and cannot see themselves using a given strategy. (Checklists provide a way to check in with teachers and assess whether they are understanding how the strategy works and if it is clear how they could use it.)
3. Coaches don't know what it looks like when they're explaining strategies, and they may think they're being completely clear and concise when they are not. A video can reveal this, and using an appropriate checklist while reviewing the video provides focus and helps guard against false clarity.
4. Checklists help a coach remember everything by providing a clear structure and map for explaining the teaching strategies to teachers.

Checklists challenge coaches to describe a practice concisely and help them get to the core of a strategy by identifying the essential elements.

HINTS FOR CHECKLIST USE

» Go through the checklist line by line with the teacher
» Get confirmation of understanding from the teacher
» Ask for feedback and think together with the teacher about ways to adapt the strategy to better meet students' needs
» Keep the checklists short and focused on the essential elements of a strategy so those elements are easy to remember

BAD CHECKLISTS

(paraphrased from *The Checklist Manifesto*, 2009)

» are vague and imprecise
» are too long
» are hard to use
» are impractical
» are made by "desk jockeys"
» assume people are dumb
» turn brains off
» clutter the page

"... What looks like resistance is often a lack of clarity."
//////////////

HEATH AND HEATH
Switch, 2010

"... Under conditions of complexity, not only are checklists a help, but they are required for success."
//////////////

ATUL GAWANDE
The Checklist Manifesto, 2009

GOOD CHECKLISTS

(paraphrased from *The Checklist Manifesto*, 2009)

» are precise
» are short but efficient, containing essential information
  (5-9 items max)
» are easy to use
» don't spell everything out
» only include critical steps
» are practical
» don't clutter the page

HOW MANY CHECKLISTS SHOULD A COACH USE?

Use as many as necessary, but as few as possible!

....

....

....

....

....

....

....

....

....

HOW TO SHARE CHECKLISTS

Checklists are used to explain new practices with precision. They are meant to facilitate dialogue between the coach and the teacher as they co-construct the lists. The process should be fun and intellectually stimulating.

1. Be precise and provisional
   » Be systematic in listing the critical steps
   » Offer the lists provisionally and ask the teacher if he or she wants or needs to modify anything; each line is a choice, not an obligation
   » Allow for iterations and local customizations of the checklist

2. Watch for "lethal mutation" (Anne Marie Palincsar)

   The coach may honestly share her thoughts on why a strategy selected by the teacher would be less effective, but in the end the teacher is empowered to practice the strategy as he or she sees fit. In other words, the accountability is to the goal, not the strategy. And if mutation of the strategy as desired by the teacher does not work, that will become clearly apparent.

   One of the most important attributes a coach must possess is patience. When the coach acknowledges that she need not force a teacher to do things the "right" way and that the proof of effectiveness will be shown by whether or not he or she is moving toward the goal, it's much easier to be relaxed and offer all the autonomy the teachers needs—even the freedom to deconstruct a strategy into useless bits. Time may be lost in the process, but that is OK because that is time spent showing respect for the teacher and her right to her own learning journey.

3. Encourage dialogue.

   Examples:
   - » "Tell me what you think about this ..."
   - » "I'm wondering about ..."
   - » "What are some ways you might teach this ..."

4. Make sure the teacher sets the goals.
   - » Be OK with the teacher's goal even if it's not what you would have chosen. Both of you might be surprised!
   - » You are not the fidelity police. If a modified practice works, then celebrate that and take notes!
   - » If the goal is not met, there's no judgment! You just keep working together to refine the goal or the practices to help achieve it.

3.

//////////////////////

Strategies Can Be Shared and Taught by Modeling

One of the most powerful ways to get the gist of an idea is to see it in action. There are five ways for a coach to show (model) a teaching strategy to a teacher: (a) modeling it in the teacher's classroom with students present, (b) modeling it in the teacher's class without the students present, (c) co-teaching it, (d) having the teacher visit another teacher's classroom, or (e) watching video of the strategy being implemented.

MODELING THE STRATEGY IN THE TEACHER'S CLASSROOM WITH THE STUDENTS PRESENT
  » Coaches don't need to teach an entire lesson—they just need to model the teaching strategy being learned.
  » If a coach teaches the entire class, it can erode a teacher's authority.
  » The goal of modeling is to make it easy for teachers to implement teaching strategies effectively.

Hints for the Coach While Preparing for the Model Lesson
  » Consider being introduced to the class as another professional who is trying out a new strategy and needs feedback from the teacher and the students. (The coach is positioned as the one who needs help, not the teacher.)
  » Make sure you have a deep understanding of the practices you will be modeling.
  » Don't try to dazzle the students; a simple, clear demonstration is all that is necessary.
  » Prior to the lesson, discuss behavioral expectations in the classroom with the teacher and confirm who will be managing students' behavior if expectations are violated. Also discuss which students have particular learning needs that should be addressed.
  » Consider having the students make name tents, so you can call on them by name.
  » Honor the collaborating teacher during the model lesson.
  » Video record the model lesson for further self-coaching and development as a coach and, perhaps, to share with other teachers who want to learn the same strategy.

Additional Hints

» Consider getting to the class early to familiarize yourself with the students and to help ease the transition to having two teachers in class.
» Review the strategy as necessary.
» Be clear about what the expectations are for the class.
» Have the students summarize what they have learned.
» Expect to learn from you collaborating teacher.

MODELING IN THE CLASSROOM WITHOUT THE STUDENTS PRESENT

» Some teachers feel more comfortable with this arrangement.
» If the teacher wants to introduce the strategy to the students, this setup allows for that.
» Modeling in front of the kids does not work well if the goal is a behavioral goal.
» Without the students present, the coach and teacher can stop the model at any point and discuss how it is going.
» Prior to any modeling, make sure the teacher has a copy of the checklist.

Using Assessments Effectively

//

USE ASSESSMENTS EFFECTIVELY TO:

○   Ensure that all students respond.

○   Develop a group response ritual.

○   Ask students to explain their responses.

○   Use effective questioning techniques.

○   Reinforce students as they respond.

○   Read nonverbal cues.

○   Create a mistake-friendly culture.

○   Consider giving students progress charts.

MODELING BY CO-TEACHING

» Co-teaching makes sense when a coach knows she does not have enough knowledge of the content the students are learning.
» Co-teaching allows the coach to model a teaching strategy in a particular part of a lesson while the teacher can ensure correct content is taught.
» Co-teaching is also effective when collaborating teachers are unhappy with some aspect of the lesson and would like the coach's help or advice during or after the lesson.

Co-Teaching Hints and Helps

» The partnership principle of equality is clear during co-teaching, with the teacher and the coach sharing authority.
» To ensure co-teaching works well and the lesson goes smoothly, consider using the Co-Teaching Planning Form included here.

MODELING BY VISITING ANOTHER TEACHER'S CLASSROOM

» Can help the teacher master all kinds of strategies.
» Can help the teacher understand how to implement broader approaches to learning or new instructional programs.
» Ideally, the coach, teacher and model teacher meet after the class to discuss what they saw.
» In order for your collaborating teachers to visit other classrooms, you (the coach) may need to offer to cover classes for them.
» Everything we know about learning from modeling applies here, including: (a) everyone (the coach, collaborating teacher, and model teacher) should review a checklist for the teaching strategy prior to class; (b) everyone should meet after the lesson to discuss what happened; and (c) if everyone agrees, a video recording of the lesson can be a valuable learning tool the collaborating teacher and the model teacher create to add to a library of model lessons that other teachers can learn from.

Co-Teaching Plan

LOCATION   DATE   TIME

TOPIC

GOAL

TIME	YOU	ME

About Model Teachers
- » Model teachers need to be masters of the strategies they are demonstrating.
- » Model teachers must be confident and at ease discussing what goes on in their class.
- » Model teachers need to be positive and emotionally intelligent.

Notes for the Coach
- » At the start of the school year, look for and cultivate model teachers.
- » Create a schedule of when strategies will be in use in model teachers' classrooms and keep that handy for quick reference.
- » Consider creating a video library of the model teachers demonstrating the strategies to be used as needed.
- » Consider partnering with one or two teachers to create model classrooms.

MODELING BY WATCHING VIDEO
- » Video is a useful aid for modeling, reviewing, and learning new strategies as well as for continued self-coaching for the model teacher.
- » Consider creating a library of modeling videos to accompany your Instructional Playbook.
- » Take advantage of online video libraries of modeled strategies as found at The Teaching Channel.

There is enormous value in seeing a strategy modeled in several different ways. The more we see things in different contexts, the more we learn.

MAKING IT REAL
- » Create a coaching community (or professional learning community) for support and help in deepening coaching skills.
- » Create checklists with a team of coaching colleagues.
- » Video record yourself describing teaching strategies to collaborating teachers and analyze each video for simplicity, clarity, and content. (This type of video coaching may also be done together with your coaching team/professional learning community/or a peer coach).

GOING DEEPER

What books listed in *The Impact Cycle* Going Deeper section might you or your coaching community study?

Atul Gawande's (2011) *The Checklist Manifesto: How to Get Things Right*

Joseph Grenny, Kerry Patterson, David Maxfield, and Ron McMillan's (2013) *Influencer: The New Science of Leading Change, Second Edition*

John Hattie, *(2012) Visible Learning for Teachers: Maximizing Impact on Learning*

Robert Marzano, (2007) *The Art and Science of Teaching: A Comprehensive Framework for Effective Instruction* (2007)

John Saphier, Mary Ann Haley-Speca, and Robert Gower, (2008) *The Skillful Teacher: Rebuilding Your Teaching Skills, 6thEdition*

Randy Sprick, (2009) *CHAMPS: A Proactive and Positive Approach to Classroom Management, 2nd Edition*

Grant Wiggins and Jay McTighe, (2005) *Understanding by Design* (2005)

Jan Chappuis, (2014) *Seven Strategies of Assessment for Learning (2nd Edition)*

....
....
....
....
....
....
....
....
....
....
....
....
....
....
....
....
....

Improve:

MEASURING AND PLANNING FOR IMPROVEMENT

Identify ①

Learn ②

③ Improve

CHAPTER

////////////////////

5

"The Improve stage is where ideas turn into action, where real improvements do or do not occur. Improve is the most challenging phase of coaching since it demands a high level of imaginative brain power from teacher and coach who think together to improve the learning and well-being of students. The foundation for coaching is laid in Identify and Learn, but the learning gets real during Improve."

////////////////////

The Impact Cycle, 2017

After we have a clear picture of reality, have set a PEERS goal, and have identified and learned strategies we believe will help us reach the goal, we are ready to enter the last phase of the Impact Cycle: Improve. This is where the magic happens! We suggest you keep a clear focus on the goal, stay patient and open-minded, and let the fun—and change!—begin.

During the Improve phase, the coach and teacher move through the following four steps: (a) Confirm Direction, (b) Review Progress, (c) Invent Improvements, and (d) Plan Next Actions.

The question addressed in the Improve phase is ...

Did we hit the goal?

If the answer is yes, ask the collaborating teacher ...
   » Do you want to continue to refine your use of the practice?
   » Do you want to choose a new goal to work on?
   » Do you want to take a break?

If the answer is no, ask the collaborating teacher ...
   » Do you want to change the goal?
   » Do you want to change the way you measure progress toward the goal?
   » Do you want to stick with the strategy as is?
   » Do you want to revisit how you teach the strategy?
   » Do you want to choose a new strategy?

Step 1
//////////////////////

Confirm Direction

When a coach and teacher meet to discuss progress toward the goal, the first thing to do is to unpack the collaborating teacher's most pressing concerns by asking questions.

Two questions are especially helpful for confirming the direction for the coaching conversation:

1. Given the time we have today, what's the most important thing for us to talk about? (Susan Scott, *Fierce Conversations*, 2004)
   » This question positions the teacher as the one setting the agenda.
   » It ensures issues that are important to the teacher are addressed.

2. What's on your mind? (The Kickstarter Question, Michael Bungay Stanier, *The Coaching Habit*, 2016)
   » The Kickstarter Question helps confirm direction quickly by getting to the heart of the matter.
   » It helps move the session naturally to step two: Review Progress.

Step 2

//////////////

Review Progress

During instructional coaching, there are primarily two reasons why data are gathered: (a) to assess how close students are to the goal to identify what adjustments need to be made in order to ensure the goal is hit; and (b) to help gauge how the teacher is implementing the new strategy.

If goals have been met, the coach and teacher plan their next actions. If the goal has not been met, they can move through the following series of questions (as appropriate to the coaching situation) to take a deeper look at what the data reveal.

A. What has gone well?
   » This question begins on a positive note!
   » Ask: Can this success be amplified or applied to other aspects of the lesson in some way?
   » Other ways to ask this question are: "What are you seeing that shows this strategy is successful?" and "What progress has been made toward the goal?"

B. What did you learn?
   » This is an open-ended question, but it still provides some focus for the conversation.
   » It highlights the iterative, experimental, and creative nature of the work teacher and coach are doing together.
   » Another way of asking this question is: "What surprised you?"

C. What roadblocks are you running into?
   » This question helps balance the highs and lows of the coaching cycle.
   » It is open-ended, which encourages dialogue.
   » The question helps focus the teacher's commitment to the goal by asking, "What would it look like if your students cared deeply and were highly engaged in their learning?"
   » After discussing what that would look like, ask: "What could we do that might move the students in that direction?"

Step 3

//////////////////

Invent Improvements

During instructional coaching, most changes are made to address challenges that surface in the improvement stage, and the kind of challenges faced are usually technical or adaptive. This is important because different kinds of challenge requires a different response. In fact, As Ron Heifetz and Marty Linsky explain in *Leadership On The Line: Staying Alive Through The Dangers of Leading* (2002) when you fail to respond to a certain type of task or challenge in the correct manner, you set yourself up for failure.

KINDS OF TASKS
(Glouberman and Zimmerman, 2002)
  » Simple: Task involves simple steps; same results each time (e.g., baking a cake).
  » Complicated: Task involves more complicated formulas and recipes but still offers a predictable outcome (e.g., putting someone on the moon).
  » Complex: Task cannot be broken down into steps with predictable outcomes; every day is different (e.g., raising a 3-year-old).

Different types of challenges require different and appropriate responses.

Simple and complicated tasks produce what Heifetz and Linsky call technical challenges. A technical challenge has known solutions. Usually, people successfully address technical challenges by following a certain set of steps or a recipe.

Complex tasks produce what Heifetz and Linsky call adaptive challenges. These require adaptive responses. There is no how-to manual for responding to these tasks. You have to be creative, imaginative, and be adaptive enough to make it up as you go. As Ron Heifetz states, "Making progress requires going beyond any authoritative expertise to mobilize discovery, shedding certain entrenched ways, tolerating losses, and generating new ideas to thrive anew (2002)."

Teaching is a complex task that requires endless adaptability!

"The most common failure in leadership is produced by treating adaptive challenges as if they were technical problems."
//////////////////

HEIFETZ AND LINSKY
Leadership on The Line, 2002

THE FIVE QUESTIONS FOR ADAPTIVE PROBLEM SOLVING

Instructional coaches need to be adaptive problem solvers. Asking the following five questions can help:

1. Do you want to stick with the strategy as it is?
   - » Change doesn't happen immediately, and sometimes things stay the same—or get worse—before they get better. Have you given the strategy enough time?
   - » Sometimes it takes a while for students to become more engaged and responsive to the new way of doing things. Are the students used to operating this way yet?
   - » In short, does the strategy need more time to have an impact, or is it clearly not facilitating progress toward the goal?

2. Do you want to revisit the way you use the strategy?
   - » Further adaptation may be needed to refine the strategy for maximum impact. Consider the following three ideas:
     - The teacher may need to change her practice;
     - The teacher may determine that the modifications she made to the strategy decreased the strategy's effectiveness; or
     - The teacher may decide that more changes need to be made in order to increase the strategy's impact.

3. Do you want to choose a new strategy?
   - » Remember: Everything is an experiment! Relatively speaking, some strategies may work better than others.
   - » If the teacher decides to change the strategy, the coach should repeat most parts of the Learn phase of the Impact Cycle (checklists, adaptations, and modeling).

4. Do you want to change the way you measure progress toward the goal?
   - » An effective measure is valid and reliable, and yields the same score when used by different people.

5. Do you want to change the goal?

   - » A general goal provides a rough target and gets the coaching cycle moving, but once changes and strategies are implemented, it may become clear that the goal needs to be refined or changed altogether.
   - » Consider: The goal may be too challenging or not challenging enough; also, it may not take the standards into account.

"Coaching is informed, adaptive response."
//////////////
The Impact Cycle, 2017

» Caution: Resist the temptation to choose less challenging goals before you are absolutely certain the goal needs to be modified.

Step 4
//////////////

Plan Next Actions

As teachers move through the Impact Cycle, there will be highs, and there will be lows. Collaborating teachers may find themselves frustrated and discouraged. This is a normal part of change. It is this feeling that Michael Fullan (*Leading In A Culture of Change*, 2001) and Seth Godin (*The Dip*, 2007) refer to as The Implementation Dip, or more simply, The Dip.

THE DIP

Moran and Lennington have identified five phases people typically go through when they are making changes: (a) uninformed optimism, (b) informed pessimism, (c) the valley of despair, (d) informed optimism, and (e) success and fulfillment.

Instructional coaches guide teachers through the valley of despair. The Dip may involve dips in confidence or performance, as well as anxiety, fear, confusion, and feelings of being overwhelmed or incompetent.

Coaches help guide teachers through these rough patches by ...
  » confidently and calmly helping them stay focused on the goal
  » pointing out gains already made
  » reminding them that change is messy. A coach is a living, breathing assurance: "It's OK. We can do this!"
  » helping identify ways to get over roadblocks

PLANNING IN COACHING

A rule of thumb: Too much planning is better than too little!

Making a plan for next actions with your collaborating teacher involves four steps:
  » Establish the date and time for the next meeting.
  » Identify which tasks need to happen before the meeting.
  » Identify who will do which tasks.
  » Estimate when the tasks will be completed.

The Coaching Planner included below can be especially helpful at this stage.

Here are some hints for how to use the form.
- » Use the form when you are meeting the teacher to plan next actions.
- » Complete the form from left to right.
- » Use it while moving through the four steps of the Improve Questioning phase or with teachers after they have worked through those questions.

Coaching Planning

GOAL	PROGRESS	NEXT ACTIONS	WHEN	COMMITMENT LEVEL (1-5)
○	○			
○	○			
○	○			
○	○			
○	○			
○	○			
○	○			

As you work through the planning form, consider the following:

1. Does the goal need modifying? If yes, write a new goal.
2. Have you modified the goal? If so, record the latest data on progress toward the goal.
3. Consider identifying the next actions by writing them down on sticky-notes. Then, organize the stickies chronologically, and identify who will do what.
4. Partner with the teacher to determine a realistic completion date. As always, the collaborating teacher is the decision maker here.
5. Ask the collaborating teacher about her commitment to the goal. You could use a scale of 1-10 with 10 being I'm still very committed and 1 being I'm totally done with this goal. If a teacher's commitment has decreased, consider revisiting the Invent Improvements step and make adaptations until the teacher feels the goal is worth the effort.

MAKING IT REAL

Continue to select key coaching conversations to video record so you can self-coach by analyzing your questioning skills.

How are you doing at fighting the urge to give advice?

....
....
....
....
....
....
....
....
....

How are you doing at relaxing into the goal and allowing it to be the driver of accountability instead of feeling like you have to advise, push, force, or worry?

....
....
....
....
....
....
....
....
....

GOING DEEPER

What books or forms of learning will you (with or without a coaching team) tackle next?

....
....
....
....
....
....
....
....
....

NOTES

....
....
....
....
....
....
....
....
....
....
....
....
....
....
....
....
....
....
....
....
....
....
....
....
....
....

CHECKLIST:

Impact Cycle

//

IDENTIFY:

○ Teacher gets a clear picture of current reality by watching a video of their lesson or by reviewing observation data (video is best!).

○ Coach asks the identify questions with the teacher to identify a goal.

○ Teacher identifies a student-focused goal.

○ Teacher identifies a teaching strategy to use to hit the goal.

LEARN:

○ Coach shares a checklist for the chosen teaching strategy.

○ Coach prompts the teacher to modify the practice if the teacher wishes.

○ Teacher chooses an approach to modeling that they would like to observe & identifies a time to watch modeling.

○ Coach provides modeling in one or more formats.

○ Teacher sets a time to implement the practice.

IMPROVE:

○ Teacher implements the practice.

○ Data is gathered (by teacher or coach in class or while viewing video) on student progress toward to the goal.

○ Data is gathered (by teacher or coach in class or while viewing video) on teacher's implementation of the practice (usually on the previously viewed checklist).

○ Coach and teacher meet to confirm direction and monitor progress.

○ Coach and teacher make adaptations and plan next actions until the goal is met.

Appendix

WORKSHOP RESOURCES

Coaching Planning Form

//

1. What are some of the typical challenges, opportunities, issues you experience in collaborating teachers' classrooms?

....

....

....

....

....

....

....

....

....

....

COACHES QUESTIONS

» What would I see in a typical classroom in your school?

» And what else?

2. What is a PEERS goal that might address some of the challenges, opportunities, issues of one typical classroom?

....

....

....

....

....

....

....

....

....

COACHES QUESTIONS

» What can be done to make this goal more Powerful, Easier, More Emotionally Compelling, More Reachable (measureable— we'll discuss teaching strategies later).

» Should anything be changed to make this goal more clearly student-focused?

3. What is a teaching strategy that might help teachers hit
   their goal?

....

....

....

....

....

....

....

....

....

....

COACHES QUESTIONS

» Find two or three strategies in The Instructional Playbook and
   ask, "Could any of these be used by the teacher to hit the goal?"

4. How can you describe that teaching practice using a checklist?

....

....

....

....

....

....

....

....

....

....

....

....

COACHES QUESTIONS

» Ask, what can be done to the checklist to make it more concise,
   explicit, precise, easy to understand, and more comprehensive?

5. How will you model the teaching practice?

....
....
....
....
....
....
....
....
....
....
....

COACHES QUESTIONS

» Ask what approach to modeling (in the class, co-teaching, modeling without students, visiting another classroom, watching
video) will be most attractive to teachers? Which approach will
most help teachers learn the teaching strategy? Should you
provide more than one model?

6. How will you move through the Improve stage of coaching?

....
....
....
....
....
....
....
....
....
....
....
....
....

COACHES QUESTIONS

» How often will you meet? How will you go about confirming
direction, monitoring progress, inventing improvements, planning next actions?

Additional Resources

///////////////////

» instructionalcoaching.com

» radicallearners.com

» facebook.com/instructional.coaching

» corwin.com/highimpactinstruction

» corwin.com/focusonteaching

» resources.corwin.com/knightbetterconversations

» resources.corwin.com/impactcycle

A SAGE Publishing Company

Helping educators make the greatest impact

CORWIN HAS ONE MISSION: to enhance education through intentional professional learning.

We build long-term relationships with our authors, educators, clients, and associations who partner with us to develop and continuously improve the best evidence-based practices that establish and support lifelong learning.

Solutions you want. Experts you trust.
Results you need.

AUTHOR CONSULTING

Author Consulting

On-site professional learning with sustainable results! Let us help you design a professional learning plan to meet the unique needs of your school or district. www.corwin.com/pd

INSTITUTES

Institutes

Corwin Institutes provide collaborative learning experiences that equip your team with tools and action plans ready for immediate implementation. www.corwin.com/institutes

eCOURSES

eCourses

Practical, flexible online professional learning designed to let you go at your own pace. www.corwin.com/ecourses

READ2EARN

Read2Earn

Did you know you can earn graduate credit for reading this book? Find out how: www.corwin.com/read2earn

Contact an account manager at (800) 831-6640 or visit **www.corwin.com** for more information.